The Power of a Teacher

BY
Tonya Winfield

"The Power of a Teacher: Shaping Lives and Futures"

Dedication

To all the teachers who give of themselves so selflessly—
who inspire with kindness, lead with patience, and teach with love.

To those who see potential where others may not,
who lift up their students and encourage dreams,
and who create a legacy of hope and possibility with every lesson.

This book is dedicated to you, the everyday heroes shaping lives and futures.

"The Power of a Teacher: Shaping Lives and Futures"

Introduction

- **Purpose**: The lasting influence of teachers on individual lives and the world.
- **Contents**:
    - Why teaching is more than just a profession—it's a calling that shapes futures.
    - Goal: to inspire readers by highlighting the critical role of teachers.

Chapter 1: The Role of a Teacher in Society

- **Purpose**: How teachers contribute to society by developing informed, compassionate citizens.
- **Contents**:
    - How teachers foster societal growth through education.
    - The moral and social responsibilities teachers take on.
    - Examples of how great teachers contribute to the community beyond academics.
    - Research and data on the economic and social impact of education led by dedicated teachers.

Chapter 2: The Emotional Impact of Teachers on Students

- **Purpose**: Explore the emotional bonds and trust that teachers build with students.
- **Contents**:
    - Discuss how positive relationships with teachers can boost students' self-esteem and confidence.
    - Stories of teachers who inspired students through emotional support.
    - Insights on empathy, patience, and understanding as critical traits for impactful teaching.
    - Research on how emotional support from teachers affects students' resilience, motivation, and success.

Chapter 3: Academic Influence and Life-Long Learning

- **Purpose**: Examine how teachers inspire a love of learning and curiosity in students.
- **Contents**:
    - The importance of instilling critical thinking, creativity, and a passion for learning.
    - Stories of teachers who went beyond the curriculum to spark curiosity.
    - Practical ways teachers can encourage life-long learning habits.
    - Research on long-term educational outcomes influenced by dedicated teachers.

Chapter 4: Overcoming Challenges: The Resilience of Teachers

- **Purpose**: Address the challenges teachers face and their resilience in overcoming them.
- **Contents**:
    - Common challenges in teaching: limited resources, large class sizes, diverse learning needs.
    - Inspirational stories of teachers persevering through tough situations.
    - The role of teacher communities and self-care in maintaining resilience.
    - Emphasize the rewards that come with overcoming these challenges.

Chapter 5: The Legacy of a Teacher's Influence

- **Purpose**: Illustrate how the impact of teachers extends beyond their time in the classroom.
- **Contents**:
    - Stories of students who have been inspired by teachers to pursue careers or passions.
    - How the lessons and values teachers impart shape students' lives.
    - Examples of former students who have honored their teachers' legacy in their own lives.
    - The ripple effect: how one teacher's impact can spread through generations.

Chapter 6: Becoming a Powerful Teacher: Tips for New Educators

- **Purpose**: Provide practical advice for new and aspiring teachers.
- **Contents**:
    - Tips on building positive relationships, maintaining enthusiasm, and finding balance.
    - Strategies for handling challenges and growing as a professional.
    - Suggestions for continuing professional development.
    - Resources and communities to support teacher growth.

Conclusion: Celebrating the Power of Teachers

- **Purpose**: Summarize the book's themes and reinforce the importance of teachers.
- **Contents**:
    - Recap the essential role teachers play in society.
    - A call to action for current and future educators to embrace their potential impact.
    - Appreciation for teachers' dedication and the lasting difference they make.

Introduction: The Heart of a Teacher's Journey

Teaching is one of the most powerful acts of human connection, and its impact reaches beyond textbooks, exams, and classrooms. Every day, teachers walk into their classrooms with the ability to shape not just minds, but lives. The quiet influence of a teacher is profound and lifelong, weaving into the personal stories of each student they meet. This book, *The Power of a Teacher: Shaping Lives and Futures*, is a tribute to that influence.

We may remember a teacher who believed in us before we could believe in ourselves, who saw potential where we saw none. For many, teachers are the first adults outside of family to show unwavering support, encouragement, and even a vision for what we could become. They are mentors, coaches, and sometimes, lifelines. And beyond personal growth, teachers lay the foundation for a better society by nurturing informed, responsible, and compassionate citizens.

Why Teaching is More Than a Profession

Teachers are often seen as providers of knowledge, but the true scope of their role goes far deeper. They don't just transfer information; they guide, challenge, and inspire. A teacher's work is as much about character-building as it is about academic achievement. Whether instilling resilience, fostering curiosity, or modeling empathy, teachers help shape the whole person. This is a profession that requires dedication, resilience, and a profound commitment to others' growth.

When a teacher encourages a struggling student to try one more time, their influence may ripple forward, eventually changing the student's perception of themselves and their potential. A simple lesson on critical thinking or respect for others can profoundly impact how a student interacts with the world for the rest of their life. These are moments that do not always make it onto report cards or into graduation ceremonies, yet they represent the true power of teaching.

The Purpose of This Book

The goal of *The Power of a Teacher: Shaping Lives and Futures* is to recognize and celebrate the incredible impact that teachers have on individual lives and society at large. Each chapter is designed to explore different facets of a teacher's role—from the emotional bonds they form with students, to the academic and lifelong learning habits they instill, to the legacy of their work that extends far beyond their classroom walls.

Through stories, insights, and practical examples, this book will explore the countless ways that teachers leave their mark. It's also a guide for both new and experienced teachers, offering inspiration and strategies to make their own teaching as impactful as possible. By understanding and celebrating this profession's depth and breadth, we hope to inspire a new generation of teachers and remind all educators of the incredible power they hold.

What You'll Discover

In the following chapters, we will look at how teachers contribute to society, the emotional connections they form, and the resilience they need to overcome challenges. We'll examine the unique challenges and triumphs of teaching, diving into the stories of those who have transformed classrooms and lives. And for aspiring educators, we'll provide practical tips on making their journey in education as impactful as it can be.

Ultimately, *The Power of a Teacher* is a book of gratitude and recognition for those who dedicate their lives to others' growth. It is a celebration of the everyday heroes whose influence extends far beyond what they might ever see. For without teachers, there would be no doctors, engineers, artists, or scientists. This is the heart of teaching—a calling that truly has the power to shape lives and futures.

Chapter 1: The Role of a Teacher in Society

Teachers hold an extraordinary place in society, as they nurture not just academic knowledge but the skills, values, and character traits that shape future generations. When we think of societal progress—whether it's advancements in technology, health, environmental sustainability, or social justice—there's often a teacher behind the inspiration. This chapter explores the vast role of teachers, extending beyond the four walls of a classroom, and delves into how they empower individuals, communities, and society at large.

1.1 Teachers as Builders of Society

Societies are built on shared knowledge, common values, and collective goals—all of which are first encountered in classrooms. Teachers are the architects of this foundation, educating students on both practical skills and social responsibilities. They play a key role in:

- **Fostering Critical Thinking**: By encouraging students to question, evaluate, and reason, teachers nurture critical thinkers who can analyze issues, challenge injustices, and propose solutions.
- **Promoting Empathy and Inclusion**: In diverse classrooms, teachers promote respect and understanding across cultures, abilities, and backgrounds, laying the groundwork for a more inclusive society.
- **Inspiring Civic Responsibility**: Through lessons on history, ethics, and current events, teachers help students understand their role in society and the impact they can have as active citizens.

In every country and culture, teachers are instrumental in creating informed, responsible citizens. Their influence directly shapes a society's potential for empathy, unity, and progress.

1.2 Moral and Social Responsibilities of Teachers

While teachers deliver academic content, their responsibilities extend to instilling ethical values and social norms that are crucial for a cohesive society. Teachers often model respect, kindness, resilience, and fairness, setting a standard that students carry into their own lives. These moral lessons include:

- **Integrity and Honesty**: By demonstrating honesty in their actions and accountability in their words, teachers instill these values in students, who, in turn, take them into their communities.
- **Resilience and Hard Work**: Teachers often show students that effort and perseverance lead to progress. These traits are crucial, especially in an age where instant gratification is common. Teachers cultivate a work ethic in students that becomes valuable in the workforce and in their personal lives.
- **Fairness and Equity**: In any classroom, students have varying needs, strengths, and learning styles. Teachers who manage these differences fairly create environments where all students feel valued, fostering a sense of equity that students carry forward.

These values become part of a student's character, shaping how they contribute to society and interact with others throughout their lives.

1.3 Teachers as Community Leaders

Teachers often take on roles beyond academics, becoming vital parts of the communities they serve. Whether they're organizing school events, advocating for resources, or creating outreach programs, teachers are often community leaders who strengthen societal bonds. Here are a few ways they do this:

- **Bridging Gaps**: In many communities, teachers are one of the few consistent presences in a child's life. They help connect families to resources, support services, and community organizations, especially in areas where resources may be scarce.
- **Providing Mentorship**: Teachers often mentor students through challenging personal situations, acting as trusted guides when family members or friends may not be able to provide support. They become advocates for students, encouraging them to pursue dreams and goals they may not have thought possible.
- **Fostering Community Pride**: Teachers who engage in community activities, like hosting school events or organizing charity drives, inspire pride and a sense of belonging among students. By participating in community life, they model for students the importance of giving back, creating a cycle of positive contribution that extends beyond the school.

These roles underscore the importance of teaching as not only an academic profession but also a social one that supports the health and progress of entire communities.

1.4 The Economic and Social Impact of Education

The impact of teachers also has economic and social dimensions. Education is one of the most powerful tools to reduce poverty, bridge inequality, and drive national progress. Teachers play a pivotal role in this process by:

- **Boosting Economic Mobility**: Education opens doors to better job opportunities and higher earnings. By ensuring students are prepared for the workforce, teachers help reduce poverty and increase economic mobility.
- **Supporting Innovation and Growth**: The world's greatest innovators, leaders, and thinkers often credit teachers for sparking their curiosity and drive. When teachers inspire students, they fuel the creativity that drives industries, science, and technology forward.
- **Building a Safer Society**: Studies consistently show that higher levels of education correlate with lower crime rates. By providing meaningful guidance and a constructive path, teachers help students channel their energy into positive pursuits, reducing negative behaviors and creating safer communities.

1.5 A Teacher's Legacy in Society

The legacy of teachers is long-lasting, as they empower each generation to overcome challenges, pursue ambitions, and contribute to society. For each student who succeeds in their chosen field, who chooses to be kind, or who champions social justice, a teacher's influence is present. Teachers instill a vision of what the future can be, one student at a time.

Every time a student remembers the encouragement of a teacher, applies a lesson learned in class, or passes on a value to their own children, the teacher's legacy lives on.

Teachers truly shape the world by shaping lives—one lesson, one word of encouragement, and one student at a time.

Closing Thoughts on the Role of Teachers in Society

Teachers are not only educators but also role models, leaders, and champions of progress. Their dedication and vision help students realize their own potential, creating ripple effects that extend to the community, the nation, and beyond. Recognizing and supporting teachers' roles in society is critical because when we invest in teachers, we invest in our collective future.

Chapter 2: The Emotional Impact of Teachers on Students

Education is not only about academic achievement; it's also deeply rooted in emotional connection and personal growth. Teachers play a crucial role in fostering emotional well-being in their students. For many young people, the trust and support found in a positive student-teacher relationship can provide the encouragement needed to overcome personal challenges and unlock their potential. This chapter delves into how teachers influence students' emotional development and how these connections create a lasting impact on students' self-esteem, resilience, and growth.

2.1 Building Trust and Connection

One of the most important aspects of a teacher's influence is the connection they build with each student. This connection is founded on trust, and it can often be a stabilizing force in a student's life, especially if they face challenges at home or in their community. Key elements that help teachers build trust and connection include:

- **Consistency**: When a teacher is consistently present and supportive, students feel secure. Consistency helps students feel valued and safe, knowing they can rely on their teacher regardless of what else is happening in their lives.
- **Empathy**: Teachers who show understanding and concern for students' feelings help students feel seen and appreciated. This empathy creates an environment where students are more willing to open up, seek guidance, and take emotional risks, like trying again after failure.
- **Patience**: Teachers often have students with diverse learning speeds and emotional needs. A teacher's patience in meeting each student where they are and allowing room for growth reinforces students' confidence in themselves and in their teacher's commitment to their success.

Through trust and connection, teachers lay the groundwork for an emotional bond that encourages students to engage, explore, and grow in ways they might not otherwise.

2.2 Fostering Self-Esteem and Confidence

The belief a teacher has in a student's abilities can profoundly affect the student's self-esteem and confidence. Teachers play a key role in helping students believe in themselves by:

- **Providing Positive Reinforcement**: Small acts of encouragement and recognition go a long way in helping students feel capable and worthy. For instance, a teacher who acknowledges a student's efforts—regardless of the outcome—reinforces the value of perseverance and builds self-worth.
- **Setting Realistic, Achievable Goals**: By setting goals that are both challenging and attainable, teachers encourage students to push themselves without becoming overwhelmed. Each accomplishment reinforces a student's confidence in their ability to tackle bigger challenges.
- **Celebrating Individual Strengths**: Every student has unique strengths and areas of growth. Teachers who take the time to identify and celebrate individual strengths help students recognize their own potential, which can increase confidence and motivation.

When students feel respected and valued, they are more willing to take on challenges, make mistakes, and learn from them. This growth mindset is essential for lifelong success and resilience.

2.3 Emotional Resilience and Overcoming Challenges

Life is filled with challenges, both in and outside of school. Teachers often become role models for resilience, demonstrating how to approach difficulties with a positive, problem-solving attitude. Some of the ways teachers nurture resilience include:

- **Modeling Problem-Solving Skills**: Teachers who approach problems constructively teach students that challenges are opportunities to learn and grow. For example, when a teacher models how to stay calm and think through solutions, students learn to apply similar strategies in their own lives.
- **Encouraging a Growth Mindset**: A growth mindset—the belief that abilities and intelligence can be developed with effort—helps students approach challenges without fear of failure. Teachers who emphasize effort over innate talent teach students that they can improve through hard work, which encourages resilience.
- **Providing a Safe Space to Fail and Try Again**: A teacher who creates a safe environment for learning and making mistakes helps students build the courage to try new things without the fear of judgment. This experience of constructive failure is key to developing resilience.

Resilience is a skill that students will carry throughout life, enabling them to face personal, academic, and professional challenges with confidence and determination.

2.4 Inspiring Lifelong Motivation and Curiosity

Teachers have a unique opportunity to inspire lifelong curiosity and motivation, instilling a love for learning that goes beyond school. When teachers cultivate a positive and engaging environment, students develop an intrinsic desire to learn, explore, and grow. Key strategies include:

- **Connecting Lessons to Real-Life Contexts**: When teachers relate subjects to students' interests or real-world situations, students are more likely to stay engaged and see the value in what they're learning. This approach fuels curiosity and makes learning feel meaningful.
- **Encouraging Student Choice**: Allowing students to make choices in their learning—whether it's selecting a book, choosing a project, or exploring a topic of interest—encourages a sense of ownership and personal investment. This autonomy supports motivation and curiosity.
- **Recognizing and Celebrating Effort**: Acknowledging the effort that students put into their learning, rather than focusing solely on the outcome, can foster a love for the process of learning. This mindset helps students find joy in discovery and growth.

Teachers who inspire curiosity help students become self-motivated learners, an asset that will benefit them in all areas of life.

2.5 Long-Term Impact: Emotional Bonds and Future Success

The emotional impact that teachers have on students often lasts a lifetime. For many individuals, memories of a supportive, encouraging teacher stay with them well into adulthood. Some former students may even cite a particular teacher as the reason they pursued a career, took a chance on a passion, or overcame a difficult period in their life. This lasting impact can be seen in:

- **Career Choices**: Many students choose careers or fields of study that were first introduced to them by a passionate teacher. For example, a student inspired by a high school biology teacher may go on to become a doctor or researcher.
- **Personal Growth and Resilience**: Students who have learned resilience and self-worth in the classroom carry these traits forward, often impacting their personal relationships, professional success, and emotional well-being.
- **The Ripple Effect of Positivity**: A teacher's influence often extends beyond their students. Students who have felt supported and encouraged by teachers are more likely to support and encourage others, creating a ripple effect of positivity that touches families, communities, and society as a whole.

Closing Thoughts on the Emotional Impact of Teachers

The emotional impact of teachers is an invaluable part of their role. When teachers invest in building trust, confidence, resilience, and curiosity, they provide students with tools that extend far beyond academics. These emotional tools become part of a student's character, equipping them to face the world with strength, compassion, and an eagerness to learn.

The teacher-student bond is a powerful one, as it influences a student's outlook, self-esteem, and aspirations. By recognizing and nurturing these emotional connections, teachers contribute immeasurably to their students' success and well-being. And while this impact may not be easily measured, its effects resonate long after students leave the classroom.

Chapter 3: Academic Influence and Life-Long Learning

Teachers are the bedrock of academic development, laying the foundation for critical thinking, curiosity, and intellectual independence in their students. While much of a teacher's role revolves around delivering curriculum content, their influence goes far beyond simply imparting facts. Through their methods, encouragement, and insights, teachers ignite a passion for learning that can last a lifetime. This chapter explores how teachers cultivate students' academic potential, foster independent thinking, and inspire an enduring love of learning.

3.1 Igniting a Passion for Knowledge

At the core of effective teaching is the ability to ignite curiosity and a genuine passion for learning. This enthusiasm can turn a subject from a set of facts into a field of endless possibilities. Teachers foster this curiosity by:

- **Making Learning Engaging and Interactive**: Lessons that go beyond lectures and involve hands-on activities, experiments, or creative projects capture students' attention and spark interest in the subject. Interactive learning helps students associate discovery with enjoyment, laying the groundwork for intrinsic motivation.
- **Connecting Curriculum to Real-World Scenarios**: When teachers illustrate how academic subjects apply to real life, students are more likely to see the relevance of what they're learning. For instance, a math teacher explaining statistics in the context of everyday finances or a history teacher connecting past events to current global issues can help students feel that their education is relevant.
- **Sharing Personal Passion**: A teacher's own enthusiasm for a subject can be contagious. When students see their teacher's excitement, they are more likely to feel intrigued and motivated to engage. Teachers who openly share why they love their subjects can inspire students to view learning as something exciting rather than merely obligatory.

When teachers successfully nurture curiosity, they plant seeds of lifelong motivation for discovery that can lead students to seek out knowledge and personal growth throughout their lives.

3.2 Encouraging Critical Thinking and Intellectual Independence

Beyond specific facts and formulas, teachers help students develop skills for critical thinking, analysis, and problem-solving. These skills are invaluable in academics, and they also equip students to navigate a complex world. Teachers encourage intellectual independence by:

- **Posing Open-Ended Questions**: Questions that require more than a "yes" or "no" answer stimulate students to think critically, analyze multiple viewpoints, and explore different solutions. For example, a teacher might ask, "What might have happened if this historical event had taken a different turn?" or "How can we approach solving this environmental issue in a new way?"
- **Allowing Space for Debate and Discussion**: Class discussions encourage students to articulate their ideas, challenge assumptions, and consider different perspectives. When students learn to express and defend their views, they develop confidence in their thinking abilities and a respect for diverse opinions.
- **Promoting Problem-Based Learning**: Giving students complex problems to solve encourages them to apply their knowledge creatively and analytically. In this process, they learn not only the subject matter but also essential skills in research, collaboration, and resilience in the face of challenges.

By fostering these abilities, teachers help students cultivate intellectual independence, empowering them to seek knowledge and think critically beyond the classroom. This approach prepares students to become informed citizens, capable of understanding and contributing to societal discussions.

3.3 Nurturing Curiosity as a Foundation for Lifelong Learning

Curiosity is the engine of lifelong learning, and teachers play a crucial role in cultivating this trait. When students are encouraged to ask questions, explore new ideas, and pursue topics that interest them, they develop a mindset that values ongoing growth. Teachers encourage curiosity by:

- **Supporting Student-Led Inquiry**: Allowing students to pursue topics of interest within a subject encourages them to take ownership of their learning. For example, in a science class, a teacher might allow students to choose their own topics for a project, such as exploring marine biology or investigating renewable energy solutions.
- **Promoting a Growth Mindset**: Teachers who emphasize that intelligence and abilities can be developed with effort foster a growth mindset in students. This mindset encourages students to see challenges as opportunities for growth rather than obstacles, motivating them to continue learning even in the face of difficulties.
- **Creating a Safe Environment for Exploration**: A classroom where students feel safe to ask questions and express curiosity without fear of judgment fosters an open and inquisitive mindset. Teachers who celebrate questions, encourage exploration, and are receptive to curiosity help students feel empowered to pursue knowledge independently.

By nurturing curiosity, teachers inspire students to become lifelong learners—individuals who approach the world with curiosity, adaptability, and a readiness to embrace new knowledge and skills.

3.4 Practical Skills for Lifelong Success

Teachers also impart essential skills that support lifelong learning and success, such as time management, organization, and effective study habits. These practical skills are critical as students advance academically and eventually enter the workforce. Teachers cultivate these skills by:

- **Teaching Study Techniques and Strategies**: Effective study habits, such as note-taking, time management, and goal-setting, equip students to approach learning in a structured, efficient way. Teachers who incorporate these techniques into their lessons help students build a toolkit for academic success.
- **Modeling Organizational Skills**: Teachers who demonstrate organization and planning in their classrooms teach students the value of preparation and structure. Encouraging students to keep track of assignments, set deadlines, and break down tasks into manageable steps fosters self-discipline and productivity.
- **Encouraging Self-Reflection and Goal-Setting**: Teachers who prompt students to reflect on their progress and set achievable goals help students develop a habit of self-assessment. This practice encourages students to take ownership of their learning, identify areas for improvement, and actively pursue their aspirations.

These skills prepare students for both academic and professional success, equipping them to meet goals, manage responsibilities, and adapt to new learning environments throughout their lives.

3.5 The Lifelong Ripple Effect of Academic Influence

The influence of a dedicated teacher can have a ripple effect that extends far beyond a student's school years. Many adults reflect on the teachers who encouraged them to follow their passions or helped them see a subject in a new light, sparking a career path or lifelong interest. This lasting impact can manifest in various ways:

- **Career Choices and Passion Projects**: Students often pursue fields introduced to them by passionate teachers. For instance, a teacher who made mathematics accessible and exciting may inspire a student to become an engineer, mathematician, or data scientist.
- **Continuing Education and Personal Growth**: Adults who experience the joy of learning early in life are more likely to seek further education and personal development opportunities, contributing to their professional and personal growth.
- **Inspiring Future Generations**: Many students, inspired by their teachers, go on to teach others—whether formally in education, through mentorship, or in community involvement. In this way, the positive influence of one teacher can extend through generations, creating a legacy of knowledge, compassion, and inspiration.

Through their dedication and passion, teachers have the power to set students on paths of lifelong learning, intellectual fulfillment, and societal contribution. Their impact becomes a part of students' lives, shaping their worldview, values, and aspirations long after they leave the classroom.

Closing Thoughts on Academic Influence and Lifelong Learning

The academic influence of teachers is invaluable, as it lays the foundation for lifelong learning and personal growth. By sparking curiosity, encouraging critical thinking, and nurturing a growth mindset, teachers empower students to take charge of their education, their careers, and ultimately, their lives. The journey of learning is never-ending, and when teachers inspire a love for this journey, they give their students one of the most enduring gifts of all.

Teachers not only teach students what to learn but, more importantly, how to learn, equipping them with the curiosity, confidence, and skills to continue growing throughout their lives. Through these contributions, teachers profoundly shape society's future—one student, one lesson, one inspiration at a time.

Chapter 4: Overcoming Challenges: The Resilience of Teachers

Teaching is often described as a "calling," but that calling comes with many challenges. Teachers face large class sizes, limited resources, diverse student needs, and often a lack of societal recognition for the critical role they play. However, their resilience—the ability to adapt, persevere, and continue inspiring students despite these difficulties—is one of their most powerful qualities. This chapter explores the common challenges teachers face and highlights the resilience and dedication they demonstrate every day.

4.1 Navigating Limited Resources

Many teachers work in environments where resources are scarce, including funding for supplies, technology, and even basic infrastructure. This scarcity can create obstacles to providing quality education, yet teachers often rise to the occasion with creativity and commitment. They overcome these resource limitations by:

- **Using Creative Solutions**: When budgets fall short, teachers often innovate, finding ways to teach complex concepts with minimal materials. For example, a science teacher might turn household items into lab tools or find ways to incorporate free, online resources into lesson plans.
- **Pooling and Sharing Resources**: Teachers frequently share materials, books, and other resources with colleagues, creating a collaborative community that supports everyone involved. Resource-sharing allows teachers to maximize what little they have to offer the best possible education.
- **Fundraising and Donor Engagement**: Some teachers go the extra mile by raising funds through

platforms like DonorsChoose or by organizing local fundraising events. By engaging with their communities and using online tools, teachers can sometimes bridge resource gaps to provide a richer learning experience for their students.

Despite the frustration that limited resources can bring, teachers' resilience and resourcefulness allow them to create effective learning environments, showing students that challenges can be met with ingenuity and teamwork.

4.2 Managing Diverse Learning Needs

Every classroom is diverse, with students who have unique abilities, learning styles, and needs. Teachers often face the challenge of tailoring their instruction to ensure that each student, regardless of background or ability, has the chance to succeed. To meet diverse learning needs, teachers employ strategies such as:

- **Differentiated Instruction**: Teachers use a variety of instructional methods—such as visual aids, hands-on activities, and technology integration—to meet students where they are in terms of comprehension and skill level. Differentiated instruction ensures that students with varying abilities can engage with the material.
- **Personalized Support**: Teachers often go out of their way to provide extra support to students who need it, whether by offering one-on-one tutoring, connecting students with resources, or meeting with parents to create individualized learning plans.
- **Building an Inclusive Classroom Culture**: A sense of belonging is essential for all students to

thrive. Teachers foster inclusivity by promoting empathy, respect, and teamwork in the classroom, helping students to support each other and appreciate diversity.

Handling diverse learning needs is challenging, but teachers' commitment to inclusivity and personalized instruction helps every student feel valued and capable.

4.3 Large Class Sizes and Limited Time

Managing large class sizes is another common challenge, as it often restricts a teacher's ability to give individual attention to students. Additionally, teachers must balance many responsibilities, from lesson planning and grading to meetings and extracurricular activities, all within limited timeframes. Despite these constraints, teachers maximize their effectiveness by:

- **Efficient Classroom Management**: Establishing clear rules, routines, and expectations helps teachers maintain order and focus in larger classes, allowing more time for learning. Effective management techniques allow teachers to maintain a productive environment even when individual attention is limited.
- **Prioritizing and Delegating**: Teachers often prioritize their time by focusing on tasks that directly benefit students' learning. Some also use peer support and classroom assistants when available, delegating small tasks to help manage the workload and meet classroom needs.
- **Using Technology for Efficiency**: Technology, from grading software to online discussion boards,

can help teachers streamline their work. Many teachers use tech tools to communicate assignments, provide feedback, and even create collaborative learning experiences.

Teachers' ability to adapt to large class sizes and time constraints highlights their resilience. By finding ways to maximize impact even when resources are stretched thin, teachers ensure that learning remains effective and engaging.

4.4 Emotional and Mental Health Challenges

Teaching is an emotionally demanding job. Teachers frequently serve not only as educators but also as mentors, counselors, and role models. This level of commitment can sometimes lead to burnout, especially when combined with stressors like standardized testing demands and administrative pressures. Teachers demonstrate resilience in these areas by:

- **Building Support Networks**: Many teachers find strength in connection with other educators, sharing experiences, advice, and encouragement. Professional learning communities and support groups allow teachers to manage stress collectively, creating a shared environment of understanding and solidarity.
- **Practicing Self-Care and Setting Boundaries**: Resilient teachers recognize the importance of self-care. Setting aside time for relaxation, maintaining healthy boundaries, and pursuing hobbies outside of work help teachers recharge and sustain their commitment to teaching.

- **Accessing Mental Health Resources**: Some schools offer mental health services and counseling for teachers, helping them cope with the emotional demands of the job. Resilient teachers advocate for themselves and seek out these resources when needed, understanding that maintaining their well-being ultimately benefits their students.

By addressing their own emotional needs, teachers are better equipped to provide steady, compassionate support to their students.

4.5 Overcoming Societal Misunderstandings and Lack of Recognition

Despite the critical role teachers play, they often face misunderstandings or undervaluation from society. Teachers may encounter stereotypes, such as the belief that teaching is "easy" or that teachers work short hours, which undermines the dedication and hard work they put into their jobs. Teachers counter these challenges through:

- **Advocacy and Education**: Many teachers actively advocate for their profession, helping the public understand the complexities and demands of teaching. This may include engaging in community discussions, speaking to parents, or even participating in media opportunities to highlight the realities of teaching.
- **Building Relationships with Parents and Communities**: Teachers can overcome misunderstandings by building positive relationships with parents and community members. Regular communication, open dialogue, and

involvement in community activities help foster appreciation and support for the teaching profession.
- **Staying Focused on the Mission**: Despite the lack of recognition, resilient teachers stay motivated by focusing on their mission: educating, empowering, and inspiring the next generation. By remembering their purpose, teachers find strength to persist through societal challenges.

Overcoming these misunderstandings is an ongoing process, but by raising awareness and staying committed, teachers continue to make a difference and garner respect for the essential work they do.

Closing Thoughts on the Resilience of Teachers

Resilience is one of the most defining traits of a teacher. Each challenge they face, from resource limitations to societal misunderstandings, becomes an opportunity to innovate, advocate, and grow. Their dedication and ability to adapt showcase a resilience that inspires both students and colleagues alike.

Teachers' resilience not only sustains their work but also serves as a powerful model for students. When students see their teachers persevere, they learn about grit, determination, and the importance of persistence in the face of challenges. These are lessons that extend far beyond academics, equipping students with the resilience they need for life.

The resilience of teachers is a testament to their passion and dedication. It reminds us that while teaching may be a challenging path, it is one filled with purpose, impact, and the unwavering strength to continue shaping lives—even when the path is difficult.

Chapter 5: The Legacy of a Teacher's Influence

The influence of a teacher extends far beyond the classroom. Every lesson, act of encouragement, and moment of guidance leaves a lasting impact on students, shaping who they are and who they will become. Teachers create legacies, not only through their direct influence on individual lives but through the ripple effect that spreads across communities and generations. This chapter explores how the values, knowledge, and confidence that teachers instill leave an enduring legacy, impacting students long after they've left the classroom.

5.1 Inspiring Future Careers and Passions

For many students, a teacher's passion for their subject sparks a lifelong interest or even a career path. When teachers show genuine enthusiasm, they inspire students to see new possibilities and discover talents they may not have known they had. Teachers inspire future careers and passions by:

- **Introducing Students to New Fields**: Teachers often expose students to fields they might not encounter elsewhere. A chemistry teacher might inspire a student to become a scientist, while an art teacher might encourage a budding artist. Through their knowledge and enthusiasm, teachers introduce students to careers and hobbies that can shape their lives.
- **Encouraging Students to Pursue Their Talents**: Teachers who take the time to recognize and encourage students' unique abilities make a lasting impact. For example, a student who loves writing may be inspired to become an author, journalist, or poet through the support of a teacher who believes in their talent.
- **Fostering a Love for Learning**: Beyond specific subjects, teachers who foster a love for learning encourage students to become lifelong learners. This love of learning often translates into personal growth, intellectual curiosity, and a drive to continue exploring new areas throughout life.

Through their passion and encouragement, teachers play a crucial role in helping students find their own passions, building a foundation that can guide career paths and personal interests for years to come.

5.2 Shaping Character and Values

Beyond academics, teachers play a vital role in shaping students' character. They model values like integrity, empathy, respect, and resilience, guiding students to develop these qualities within themselves. Teachers influence character and values by:

- **Modeling Kindness and Empathy**: When teachers demonstrate kindness and understanding, they teach students the importance of compassion and respect for others. These lessons in empathy have a lasting effect on how students treat others and contribute to their communities.
- **Encouraging Integrity and Accountability**: Teachers often set high standards for honesty and accountability, encouraging students to take responsibility for their actions. These values become part of students' personal ethics, influencing how they approach both personal and professional relationships.
- **Instilling Resilience and Perseverance**: Teachers who encourage students to persevere through challenges leave an enduring impression. By modeling resilience and providing support during difficult times, teachers help students develop the strength to face obstacles throughout life.

When teachers instill these values, they do more than prepare students for academic or career success—they prepare them to be compassionate, ethical, and resilient individuals who contribute positively to society.

5.3 Creating Lifelong Connections and Memories

The bonds that form between teachers and students can be profoundly meaningful, creating memories and connections that students carry with them for life. Some of these relationships last well beyond the school years, with students returning to thank teachers or to seek guidance as adults. Teachers create lifelong connections and memories by:

- **Providing a Safe Space**: For many students, a teacher's classroom is a place of safety and acceptance. Teachers who offer a supportive environment create lasting memories, as students remember the feeling of being valued and understood.
- **Offering Unwavering Support**: Teachers who believe in their students and offer consistent encouragement become powerful figures in students' lives. These students often remember their teacher as someone who believed in them when others may not have, instilling a sense of confidence that carries them forward.
- **Celebrating Achievements and Milestones**: Teachers who celebrate students' successes—big or small—leave students with memories of feeling recognized and valued. These celebrations create a sense of pride that students remember long after they leave the classroom.

These meaningful relationships contribute to a teacher's legacy, creating memories that students cherish and often inspiring them to offer the same support and encouragement to others in their own lives.

5.4 The Ripple Effect: How One Teacher Can Impact Generations

The legacy of a teacher often extends through generations. When a teacher's influence positively shapes a student, that student may go on to make an impact on others. This ripple effect can spread through families, communities, and even society as a whole. The ripple effect of a teacher's influence can be seen in:

- **Students Becoming Role Models**: Many students who have experienced a teacher's support and guidance go on to mentor others. For instance, a student inspired by a supportive teacher might become a teacher themselves, or take on a mentorship role within their community or profession.
- **Improving Family and Community Dynamics**: The values and skills students learn from teachers often influence how they interact with their families and communities. A student who learned empathy and respect from a teacher may carry these values into their relationships, creating a positive impact on those around them.
- **Empowering Positive Social Change**: Teachers who inspire critical thinking, compassion, and a commitment to justice contribute to positive social change. Students who have been taught to question, empathize, and seek solutions often become advocates for change in their communities, contributing to a more just and compassionate society.

In this way, one teacher's legacy can extend far beyond the classroom, as students carry forward the lessons and values that contribute to a brighter future.

5.5 Honoring and Celebrating the Legacy of Teachers

While the influence of a teacher often goes unrecognized, the impact they have on society is undeniable. Teachers' legacies deserve to be celebrated and honored, both by the students they've inspired and by society at large. Honoring teachers' legacies can take many forms, such as:

- **Expressing Gratitude**: Former students who reach out to thank a teacher, even years later, give teachers a chance to see the impact of their work. Acts of gratitude remind teachers that their dedication has made a difference.
- **Creating Opportunities for Professional Growth**: When schools and communities invest in teachers' professional development, they honor the profession and support teachers in continuing to create positive legacies.
- **Recognizing Teachers as Change Makers**: By acknowledging teachers as essential contributors to society, communities can foster a greater appreciation for the teaching profession and encourage new generations to pursue this impactful career.

Honoring teachers' legacies affirms the value of their work and reinforces the understanding that their influence endures, impacting lives and shaping society for the better.

Closing Thoughts on the Legacy of a Teacher's Influence

The legacy of a teacher is woven into the fabric of students' lives, often in ways that go unseen yet profoundly shape the future. Teachers inspire passions, shape values, and create memories that last a lifetime. Their influence lives on as students carry forward the lessons, compassion, and resilience they learned, sharing these gifts with their own families, communities, and the world.

Teaching is an act of hope—a belief that each student has the potential to grow, contribute, and make a difference. In this way, teachers plant seeds that may not blossom immediately but that will eventually yield a brighter future. A teacher's legacy is a testament to their belief in the power of learning, kindness, and resilience—a lasting gift that shapes not only individuals but also the very heart of society.

Chapter 6: Becoming a Powerful Teacher: Tips for New Educators

For new teachers, the journey ahead is filled with both exciting possibilities and inevitable challenges. Teaching is a dynamic profession that calls for adaptability, empathy, and a constant commitment to growth. While each teacher's path is unique, certain strategies and practices can help new educators cultivate a strong, positive impact on their students and themselves. This chapter offers practical tips for new teachers, focusing on building relationships, fostering a love for learning, managing challenges, and achieving long-term success in the field.

6.1 Building Positive Relationships with Students

Positive student-teacher relationships are foundational to effective teaching. When students feel respected and supported, they are more motivated, engaged, and willing to take risks in their learning. Tips for building strong connections include:

- **Learning Student Names and Backgrounds**: Showing genuine interest in each student by learning their names and a bit about their interests or backgrounds fosters a sense of belonging. It also helps students feel seen and valued as individuals.
- **Practicing Active Listening**: Taking time to listen to students' thoughts and concerns shows them that their voices matter. Active listening not only builds trust but also provides valuable insights into students' unique needs and learning styles.
- **Setting Clear, Fair Expectations**: Students thrive when they know what's expected of them. Communicating classroom rules, expectations, and consequences helps create a safe environment. Fairness and consistency build trust, showing students that they are respected and valued equally.

Positive relationships set the stage for a supportive classroom environment, allowing students to feel safe, engaged, and motivated to learn.

6.2 Fostering a Love for Learning

One of the greatest gifts a teacher can give is inspiring a lifelong love of learning. When students are excited about discovery, their motivation transcends the classroom and enriches their lives. Tips for fostering a love for learning include:

- **Using Creative and Varied Teaching Methods**: Incorporating a mix of activities, such as group projects, hands-on experiments, and interactive discussions, can make learning dynamic and engaging. When students have fun while learning,

they are more likely to retain information and develop an enthusiasm for the subject.
- **Connecting Lessons to Real Life**: When students understand how what they're learning applies to real-world situations, they are more motivated to engage with the material. Relating lessons to students' interests and experiences gives meaning to their learning.
- **Encouraging Curiosity and Questions**: Creating a classroom where questions are celebrated helps students feel safe to explore new ideas. By encouraging curiosity, teachers inspire students to pursue their interests and engage in learning beyond the classroom.

Teachers who foster curiosity and excitement around learning help students develop a positive association with education, a mindset that supports lifelong growth.

6.3 Managing Classroom Challenges and Building Resilience

The teaching journey is filled with challenges, from managing diverse learning needs to adapting to limited resources. New teachers can navigate these obstacles and build resilience by:

- **Setting Realistic Goals and Expectations**: Starting with manageable goals can help prevent feelings of overwhelm. New teachers benefit from focusing on achievable objectives and celebrating small successes, which builds confidence and resilience.
- **Seeking Support from Experienced Teachers**: Veteran teachers are invaluable resources. By

seeking advice and mentorship, new teachers can gain insights into effective strategies and feel supported within their school community.
- **Practicing Flexibility and Adaptability**: Not every lesson will go as planned, and that's okay. Developing the ability to adapt and find creative solutions helps teachers respond to challenges with patience and positivity.

Building resilience takes time, but by focusing on realistic goals, seeking mentorship, and staying adaptable, new teachers can overcome challenges and continue to grow.

6.4 Developing Strong Classroom Management Skills

Classroom management is essential for creating an environment where learning can thrive. New teachers can establish a well-organized and respectful classroom by:

- **Establishing Clear Rules and Routines**: Consistent rules and routines create structure, helping students know what to expect. By involving students in creating these rules, teachers also foster a sense of ownership and responsibility.
- **Using Positive Reinforcement**: Recognizing and celebrating positive behavior encourages students to meet expectations. Positive reinforcement, like praise or small rewards, reinforces good behavior and encourages a respectful classroom atmosphere.
- **Building Relationships with Parents and Guardians**: Strong partnerships with parents can support classroom management. When parents are informed about classroom expectations, they are

more likely to support these efforts, contributing to a respectful and cohesive learning environment.

Effective classroom management supports both academic and social development, creating a space where students feel safe, respected, and ready to learn.

6.5 Embracing Professional Development and Growth

Great teachers are lifelong learners themselves. Embracing continuous growth and professional development keeps teaching fresh, effective, and fulfilling. Strategies for ongoing professional development include:

- **Participating in Workshops and Training**: Many schools offer workshops or training sessions that provide valuable strategies and insights. Whether focused on classroom management, technology integration, or subject-specific methods, these sessions offer new tools and ideas.
- **Engaging in Peer Observations**: Observing other teachers in action provides a chance to learn different techniques and approaches. Peer observations foster collaboration and allow teachers to learn from each other's strengths.
- **Setting Personal Goals for Growth**: Reflecting on personal strengths and areas for growth helps teachers set meaningful goals for improvement. Goal-setting keeps teachers motivated, focused, and aligned with their own development journey.

Investing in professional growth not only benefits teachers but also enriches their students' learning experience. A commitment to growth helps teachers stay inspired, relevant, and effective throughout their careers.

6.6 Finding Balance and Practicing Self-Care

Teaching is a demanding profession, and burnout is a real risk. Finding a healthy work-life balance and practicing self-care are essential for long-term fulfillment and effectiveness. Tips for maintaining well-being include:

- **Setting Boundaries**: Creating boundaries between work and personal life helps prevent burnout. For example, setting specific times to stop working or taking weekends off for family and rest can help teachers recharge.
- **Prioritizing Self-Care**: Making time for hobbies, exercise, and relaxation is essential for mental and emotional well-being. Self-care allows teachers to show up for their students with energy and enthusiasm.
- **Building a Support Network**: Staying connected with colleagues, family, and friends provides a strong support system. Sharing experiences and seeking encouragement can ease stress and remind teachers that they're not alone.

Self-care and work-life balance are essential for teachers to maintain their passion and effectiveness in the classroom. By caring for themselves, teachers are better equipped to care for their students.

Closing Thoughts on Becoming a Powerful Teacher

Becoming a powerful teacher is a journey of growth, discovery, and dedication. Every day offers opportunities to learn, connect, and make a difference in students' lives. By building positive relationships, inspiring curiosity, and practicing resilience, new teachers can create a lasting impact on their students and their own lives.

Teaching is a profession filled with rewards and challenges, but with the right tools, support, and mindset, it's also deeply fulfilling. New teachers who embrace the joys of learning, prioritize self-care, and continue to grow become not only effective educators but also inspirational role models. In doing so, they step into the profound power of teaching—a calling that shapes lives, futures, and society itself.

Conclusion: Celebrating the Power of Teachers

Teachers are more than educators; they are guides, mentors, and champions of possibility. In classrooms around the world, teachers are shaping lives, inspiring dreams, and creating a legacy of learning that extends beyond their own lifetime. As we've explored in this book, the impact of teachers reaches deep into students' lives, influencing their career paths, personal growth, values, and sense of self. The dedication and resilience of teachers leave a lasting mark, resonating across families, communities, and society.

The power of teaching lies in its potential to transform lives. Every day, teachers face challenges, embrace innovation, and give of themselves in ways that inspire growth and change. From fostering curiosity and resilience to providing emotional support and modeling values, teachers contribute immeasurably to the foundation of a just, compassionate, and knowledgeable world.

To those who teach—thank you. Thank you for your belief in each student, for your resilience in the face of challenges, and for the hope you bring to the future. Teaching is indeed a calling, a powerful force that shapes lives and futures with each lesson, word of encouragement, and moment of understanding. This book is a tribute to you and the transformative power of teaching.

As we honor teachers, let us also remember the legacy they leave—a legacy of empowered, curious, and compassionate individuals who carry forward the values and wisdom imparted to them. This legacy is invaluable, and it reminds us all of the power of a single teacher to make a profound difference. Teaching is not merely a profession but a gift to the world, one that shapes not only individual lives but the heart of society itself.

Journaling

Welcome to the journaling section of *The Power of a Teacher: Shaping Lives and Futures*. This collection of prompts is designed to help you reflect deeply on the inspiring themes and powerful influences explored throughout this book. Each prompt encourages you to look inward, revisit moments of learning and growth, and capture your personal journey through the lens of teaching, mentorship, and lifelong learning.

Whether you are a teacher, a student, a parent, or simply someone who has been touched by the influence of a mentor, these pages are a space for you to connect with those experiences. Here, you'll explore the impact of kindness, the transformative power of encouragement, the beauty of resilience, and the profound ways teachers and mentors shape lives.

Each prompt is followed by a page dedicated to your reflections. Take your time with each entry, allowing yourself to explore what these topics mean to you personally. As you write, remember that there are no right or wrong answers—this is your journey, your story, and your insight. Return to these pages whenever you need to reconnect with your values, celebrate your growth, or simply enjoy a quiet moment of reflection.

Let these journaling pages serve as a source of inspiration, clarity, and motivation. May they help you appreciate the remarkable journey of learning, the invaluable role of those who teach and guide, and the incredible power within you to inspire and be inspired.

1. **Reflection on Inspiration**
    - *"A great teacher sees beyond grades and looks at the heart of the student."*
    - Reflect on a teacher who inspired you. What qualities did they possess that impacted you most?

2. **The Power of Belief**
    - *"Believing in a student is the first step in helping them believe in themselves."*
    - Think about someone who believed in you when you needed it most. How did it change you?

---

3. **Leaving a Legacy**
    - *"A teacher's legacy lives on in every life they touch."*
    - Describe a quality or value you'd want your own students (or children) to remember you for.

4. **Encouraging Curiosity**
    - *"Curiosity is the engine of discovery."*
    - Reflect on a time when a teacher encouraged your curiosity. How did it shape your learning?

5. **Building Confidence**
    - *"A word of encouragement can set a life in motion."*
    - Write about a moment when a teacher, mentor, or friend lifted your confidence.

6. **Finding Your Purpose**
    - *"Teaching is more than a job—it's a purpose."*
    - What aspects of teaching (or mentoring) bring you the most fulfillment?

7. **The Gift of Patience**
    - *"True patience isn't waiting—it's understanding."*
    - Think of a teacher who showed you patience. How did it make you feel?

8. **Challenges as Opportunities**
    - *"Every challenge is a lesson in disguise."*
    - Describe a time you faced a challenge that helped you grow or gain new insight.

9. **Cultivating Kindness**
    - *"Kindness is the silent lesson that resonates long after the words fade."*
    - Write about an act of kindness from a teacher or mentor that you remember.

10. **Empowering Others**
    - *"Teaching is empowering others to believe in themselves."*
    - Reflect on a time you helped someone feel more confident or capable.

---

11. Celebrating Small Wins
- *"Each small step is a building block for future success."*
- Think about a small achievement that gave you a sense of accomplishment. What did you learn?

---

12. **The Influence of Positivity**
    - *"A positive word can change the course of a day—or a life."*
    - Describe how a positive influence has helped you through a difficult time.

---

13. **Teaching Resilience**
    - *"Resilience is the gift of never giving up."*
    - Reflect on a person who taught you resilience. What did they say or do to inspire you?

---

14. **The Joy of Learning**
    - *"Learning isn't just about knowledge; it's about joy and discovery."*
    - Write about a time when learning brought you joy.

15. **Listening with Compassion**
    - *"The best teachers listen as much as they teach."*
    - Think of a time when someone truly listened to you. How did it make you feel?

16. **Inspiration in Everyday Moments**
    - *"Great teachers find inspiration in the everyday."*
    - Reflect on a small, everyday moment that taught you something meaningful.

17. **Discovering Strengths**
    - *"Every student has a strength waiting to be uncovered."*
    - What strengths do you see in yourself today that you didn't see before?

18. **Leaving a Positive Mark**
    - *"To teach is to leave a part of yourself with others."*
    - Write about someone who left a positive mark on your life and how they did it.

19. Encouraging Curiosity in Others
- *"Curiosity is contagious."*
- Describe a way you can encourage curiosity in someone else today.

20. Perseverance in Learning
- *"Learning is a journey, not a destination."*
- Write about a lesson you learned over time, with effort and perseverance.

21. **Mentorship and Guidance**
    - *"Every guide has a guide of their own."*
    - Think of a mentor in your life. What advice did they give that you still carry with you?

22. **Celebrating Progress**
    - *"Progress is the quiet proof of perseverance."*
    - Reflect on how far you've come in your own journey of growth or learning.

23. **Seeing Potential in Others**
    - *"To teach is to see potential where others may not."*
    - Describe someone whose potential you believe in, and why.

24. **The Impact of a Single Teacher**
    - *"One teacher can change the course of a life."*
    - Write about a teacher or person who profoundly impacted your life. What was it about them?

25. **Finding Passion in Teaching**
    - *"Passion is the energy that makes teaching come alive."*
    - What aspects of teaching (or mentoring) bring you the most joy?

26. Embracing New Perspectives
- *"Learning opens minds and hearts to new perspectives."*
- Write about a time you learned something that changed the way you view the world.

27. The Power of Encouragement
- *"Encouragement plants seeds of confidence."*
- Reflect on a moment when someone's encouragement motivated you to keep going.

---

28. Teaching Life Skills
- *"Life's most important lessons often aren't in the textbooks."*
- What life skills did a teacher or mentor help you develop, and how have they served you?

29. **Overcoming Self-Doubt**
    - *"A teacher's belief can overcome a student's doubt."*
    - Think about a time someone helped you overcome self-doubt. How did it change your outlook?

---

30. Connecting with Students
- *"True connection is at the heart of every meaningful lesson."*
- Reflect on a connection you've made with a student, mentee, or child. How did it impact them?

31. Creating a Safe Learning Environment
- *"Safety is the foundation of growth."*
- Describe what makes a space feel safe to you, and how it helps you learn and grow.

32. **The Power of Storytelling**
    - *"Stories teach lessons words alone cannot reach."*
    - Think of a story someone shared with you that left a lasting impact. Why did it resonate?

33. Helping Students See Their Potential
- *"Teachers help us see the greatness we cannot see ourselves."*
- Write about someone who helped you see your own potential. How did it feel?

34. Making Learning Fun
- *"Learning thrives where joy lives."*
- What's a fun or memorable way someone helped you learn something new?

35. Setting Boundaries to Prevent Burnout
- *"To teach well, you must care for yourself well."*
- Reflect on a way you can set boundaries to protect your well-being.

36. Encouraging Resilience in Others
- *"Resilience is a gift we give through our example."*
- Write about someone you know who's shown resilience. What can you learn from their story?

37. Celebrating Individuality in the Classroom
- *"Every student is unique, every mind a world of its own."*
- Describe how embracing your individuality has helped you on your journey.

38. Teaching with Empathy
- *"Empathy is the bridge that connects us all."*
- Reflect on a time you felt truly understood by someone. How did it affect you?

39. Creating Lasting Memories in Learning
- *"Memories of a great teacher stay with us forever."*
- Think of a special memory with a teacher or mentor that still brings you joy or insight.

40. Building Confidence Through Small Wins
- *"Each small win is a step toward self-belief."*
- Write about a recent small win. How did it make you feel?

41. Fostering Curiosity in a Routine
- *"Curiosity keeps even the ordinary extraordinary."*
- How can you add a sense of curiosity to your daily routines?

42. Recognizing the Influence of Kind Words
- *"One kind word can change a day, a mind, even a life."*
- Recall a time when kind words from someone lifted your spirits.

43. **Helping Students Set Goals**
    - *"A goal is a dream with a plan."*
    - Think about a goal someone encouraged you to set and work toward. How did it impact you?

44. **Finding Beauty in Diversity**
    - *"Every student, a unique reflection of the world's diversity."*
    - Reflect on a time when diversity enhanced your learning or experience.

45. Perseverance in the Face of Difficulty
- *"Challenges are not the end but the beginning of growth."*
- Describe a challenging moment you've overcome. How did it make you stronger?

46. Recognizing Strengths in Others
- *"To recognize strength in others is to help them see it in themselves."*
- Write about someone whose strengths you admire. How do they inspire you?

47. Encouraging a Growth Mindset
- *"There is no limit to what you can learn when you believe you can grow."*
- Reflect on a time when adopting a growth mindset helped you succeed.

48. Building Connections Beyond Academics
- *"Connections built with kindness last beyond the classroom."*
- Describe a time when a teacher or mentor connected with you beyond academics.

49. Teaching Students to Appreciate Differences
- *"Differences are what make each of us unique and valuable."*
- Think about a time someone's unique perspective taught you something important.

50. **Instilling Hope for the Future**
    - *"A teacher's belief in tomorrow inspires today."*
    - Reflect on something you look forward to achieving or experiencing in the future.

51. Creating Moments of Joy in Learning
- *"Learning becomes lasting when it brings joy."*
- Write about a joyful learning experience and what made it special.

---

52. Being a Lifelong Learner
- *"The journey of learning is lifelong and ever-expanding."*
- Describe an area of knowledge you'd like to explore further.

53. Celebrating Personal Growth
- *"Growth is the quiet evolution within."*
- Reflect on how you've grown over the last year. What are you proud of?

54. Encouraging Others to Believe in Themselves
- *"The power of belief can unlock boundless potential."*
- Write about a way you can help someone believe in themselves today.

55. Learning from Everyday Heroes
- *"In every hero, there's a lesson waiting to be learned."*
- Who is an everyday hero in your life, and what have they taught you?

56. **Recognizing the Small Acts that Make a Big Difference**
    - *"Sometimes, the smallest act is the greatest gift."*
    - Reflect on a small act of kindness that left a lasting impact on you.

---

57. Celebrating Achievements, Big and Small
- *"Each accomplishment, no matter the size, is a reason to celebrate."*
- Describe a recent achievement and how you celebrated it.

58. Finding Purpose in Teaching
- *"Purpose fuels passion, and passion powers teaching."*
- Reflect on what purpose means to you in your role as a teacher or mentor.

59. Teaching Through Actions
- *"Actions speak louder than words, especially in teaching."*
- Describe a way you teach others through your actions or behaviors.

60. **Finding Strength in Community**
    - *"In community, we find support, strength, and inspiration."*
    - Reflect on a community that has supported you and what it means to you.

---

61. Embracing Lifelong Curiosity
- *"Curiosity keeps the mind and heart alive."*
- What's something new you've learned recently? How did it expand your perspective?

62. Guiding with Compassion
- *"Compassion is the guide to a connected heart."*
- Think of a time someone showed you compassion. How did it affect your outlook?

63. Recognizing the Legacy of a Teacher
- *"A teacher's legacy is written in the lives they inspire."*
- Write about a teacher or mentor whose legacy lives on in you.

64. Finding Hope in Education
- *"Education is the bridge to a brighter tomorrow."*
- Describe your hopes for the future and how education plays a role in them.

65. Celebrating the Journey of Teaching
- *"Teaching is a journey of shared discovery, growth, and joy."*
- Reflect on the journey you're on and the lessons you hope to leave with others.

I hope this book serves as a meaningful celebration of the vital role teachers play in our lives and our world!

Made in the USA
Columbia, SC
01 November 2024

7fffdc5a-3a0b-4e5f-b959-4a62aa8101a0R01